HAGFISH

by Ellen Lawrence

Consultant:
Douglas S. Fudge, PhD
Associate Professor
Schmid College of Science and Technology
Orange, California

BEARPORT PUBLISHING

New York. New York

Publisher: Kenn Goin
Senior Editor: Joyce Tavolacci
Creative Director: Spencer Brinker
Photo Researcher: Ruth Owen Books

Library of Congress Cataloging-in-Publication Data

Names: Lawrence, Ellen, 1967– author.
Title: Slime crimes : hagfish / by Ellen Lawrence.
Description: New York, New York : Bearport Publishing, [2019] | Series:
   Slime-inators & other slippery tricksters | Includes
   bibliographical references and index.
Identifiers: LCCN 2018016383 (print) | LCCN 2018020344 (ebook) |
   ISBN 9781684027415 (ebook) | ISBN 9781684026951 (library)
Subjects: LCSH: Hagfishes—Juvenile literature.
Classification: LCC QL638.14 (ebook) | LCC QL638.14 .L39 2019 (print) |
   DDC 597/.2—dc23
LC record available at https://lccn.loc.gov/2018016383

For more information, write to Bearport Publishing Company, Inc., 45 West 21st Street, Suite 3B, New York, New York 10010. Printed in the United States of America.

10 9 8 7 6 5 4 3 2 1

Contents

You've Been Slimed!

A long hagfish is wriggling through the ocean water.

A scientist swims after the eel-shaped creature to study it.

When the scientist touches the hagfish, something disgusting happens.

A thick cloud of slime bursts out of the hagfish's body!

As the scientist tries to get the goo off her hands, the fish swims away.

hagfish

How would you describe a hagfish to someone who has never seen one?

There are over 70 different kinds of hagfish. Some grow to 4 feet (1.2 m) long, while others are less than 2 inches (5 cm) long.

scientist

hagfish slime

Meet a Hagfish

A hagfish's long body is covered with loose pink, gray, or brown skin.

The fish cannot see very well.

Its simple eyes only allow it to tell light from dark.

A hagfish has one large nostril and a powerful sense of smell.

To help it find its way around, it uses feelers on its head called **barbels**.

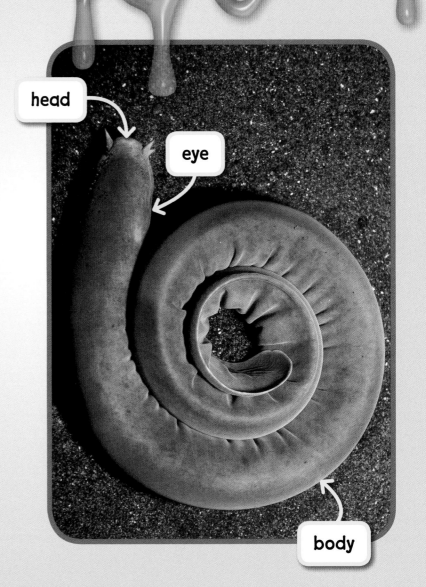

head

eye

body

Seabed Life

Hagfish live in oceans all over the world.

Most hagfish make their homes in deep, cold waters.

Some live more than a mile (1.6 km) under the ocean's surface.

A hagfish spends most of its time close to the seabed.

As it swims, it wriggles its body from side to side like a snake.

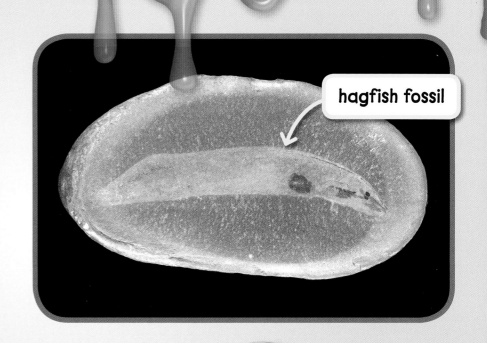

hagfish fossil

Hagfish have been on Earth for more than 300 million years. In fact, there were hagfish in the ocean at the time of the dinosaurs!

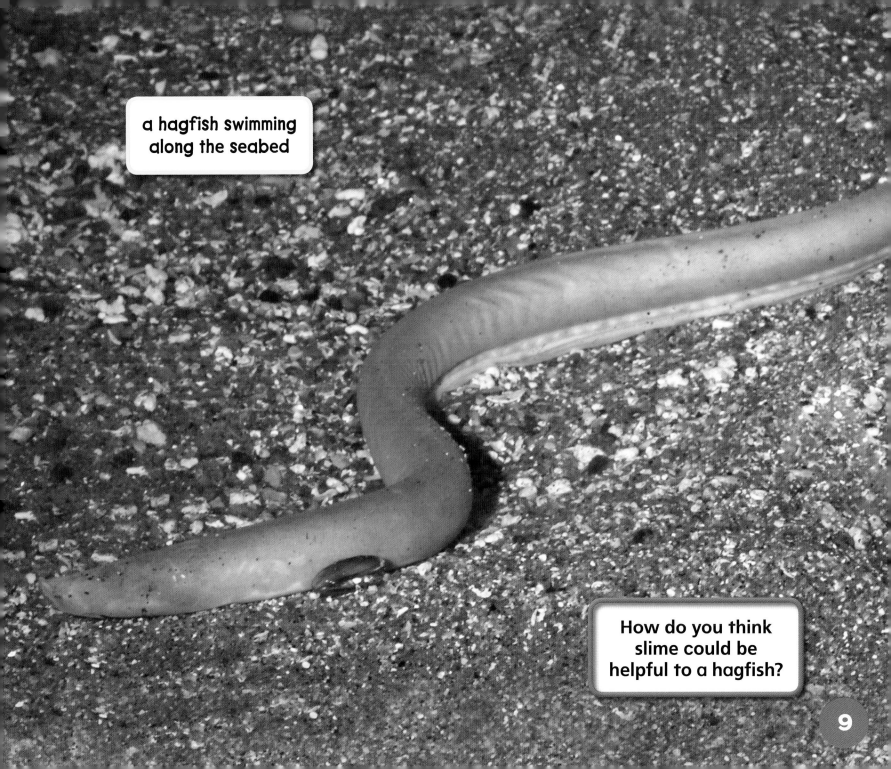

a hagfish swimming along the seabed

How do you think slime could be helpful to a hagfish?

Slime Attack

If a large fish or other predator tries to eat a hagfish, it's time for a slime attack!

A thick, whitish substance squirts from tiny holes along the sides of a hagfish's body.

As the slime mixes with the seawater, it **expands**.

The attacker then gets a big, disgusting mouthful of thick, slippery slime.

holes for slime

great white shark

gills

Even fierce sharks are afraid of hagfish slime. Sharks and other fish breathe through body parts called gills. If the sharks get slimed, the goo may block their gills, making it impossible to breathe.

Shiploads of Slime

When a hagfish is under attack, it can produce a huge cloud of slime in less than a second!

To avoid getting smothered in its own slime, a hagfish makes knots with its body.

As it unties itself, the slime is scraped off the fish's skin.

If the hagfish gets slime in its big nostril, it sneezes it out!

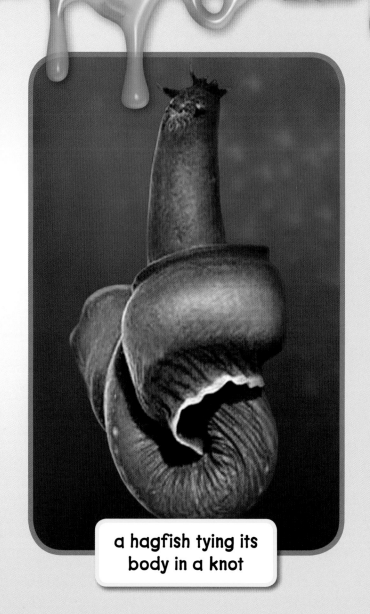

a hagfish tying its body in a knot

hagfish slime

A teaspoon of hagfish slime mixed with seawater can expand to fill a bucket in just a couple of seconds.

Let's Eat!

When it's not sliming its enemies, a hagfish searches for food.

It uses its great sense of smell and barbels to find a meal.

Sometimes, a hagfish eats small animals, such as shrimp.

Its favorite food, however, is the dead body of a shark or whale.

Once it finds a **carcass**, the hagfish buries its head in the rotting meat and starts feeding.

a hagfish about to search for food

shrimp

A hagfish gets **nutrients** from the food it eats. Scientists also believe it can soak up nutrients through its skin!

a hagfish eating a dead shark

shark carcass

Rotting Dinner

As it feeds, a hagfish chews its way deeper into a carcass.

Sometimes it enters a carcass through the dead animal's mouth, gills, or bottom!

While inside the rotting body, a hagfish keeps eating and eating.

Once it has gobbled up enough food, a hagfish can go for up to seven months without a meal!

A hagfish's mouth has a tongue-like part that contains hard, toothy **rasps**. The rasps are used for tearing flesh.

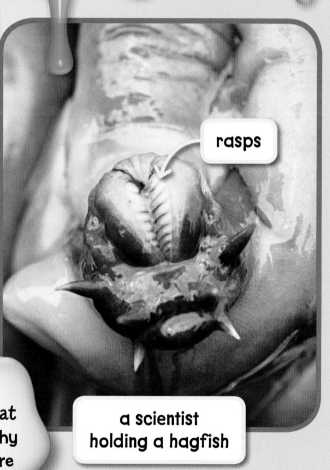

rasps

a scientist holding a hagfish

hagfish

A hagfish may seem disgusting because it feeds on dead bodies, but it's actually very helpful. Why?
(The answer is on page 24.)

Mini Slime-inators

Male and female hagfish meet up to **mate**.

The female lays up to 30 eggs.

A baby hagfish, which looks like a tiny adult, hatches from each egg.

As soon as it hatches, the baby hagfish can take care of itself.

It swims off into the ocean to grow bigger and become a super slime-inator!

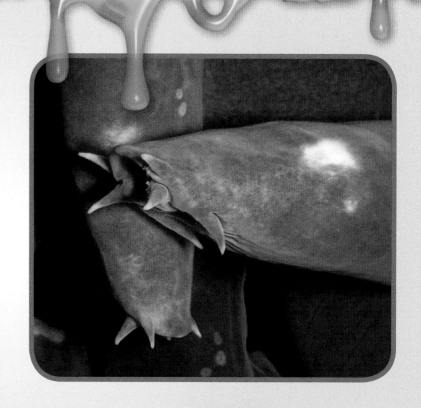

A hagfish egg is about the size of a grape.

hagfish egg

Imagine you are a scientist who has just discovered a hagfish. What name would you give to this slimy ocean creature?

19

Stringy Slime

Scientists are busy studying hagfish slime.

They've discovered that it's made up of thousands of thin, super-strong threads.

Scientists are investigating whether the threads can be used to make materials that people can use.

Maybe one day, there will be suits for scuba divers made from hagfish slime!

Some scientists are trying to make artificial, or human-made, hagfish slime. Then scuba divers could use it to protect themselves from sharks.

scientists studying
hagfish slime

Science Lab

Make Your Own Slime

Make some sticky, stretchy slime—just like a hagfish!

1. In a bowl, mix together the warm water and baking soda until the baking soda has dissolved.

2. Add the glue to the bowl and mix well.

3. Next, add the contact lens solution one tablespoon at a time. Stir the mixture until the slime forms.

4. Take the slime out of the bowl and knead it with your hands until the slime has fully formed.

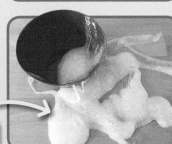

homemade slime

You will need:

- A bowl
- ¼ cup of warm water
- ½ teaspoon of baking soda
- A spoon for mixing
- 5 fluid ounces of clear Elmer's glue
- Up to 3 tablespoons of contact lens solution

Slime Investigation

- **How does the slime look, feel, and smell?**

- **Slowly push your finger into the slime and then remove it. What happens?**

- **How far can you stretch the slime?**

- **Roll the slime into a ball. What happens? Does it keep its shape?**

- **Can you think of a way to use your slime for something useful?**

Science Words

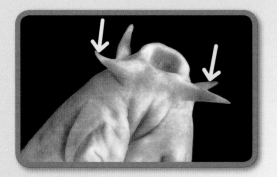

barbels (BAHR-buhlz) long, thin feelers on the heads of some kinds of fish

carcass (KAHR-kuhs) the dead body of an animal

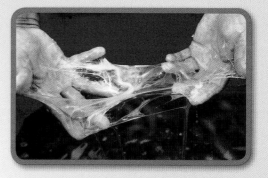

expands (ek-SPANDZ) grows bigger and takes up more space

mate (MAYT) to come together to produce young

nutrients (NOO-tree-uhnts) substances that are found in food and are needed by animals to stay healthy

rasps (RASPS) hard, tooth-like parts used for tearing or rubbing

Index

Read More

Goldish, Meish. *Disgusting Hagfish (Gross-Out Defenses).* New York: Bearport (2009).

Johnson, Rebecca L. *When Lunch Fights Back (Wickedly Clever Animal Defenses).* Minneapolis, MN: Millbrook Press (2015).

Owen, Ruth. *Disgusting Animal Defenses (It's a Fact!).* New York: Ruby Tuesday (2014).

Learn More Online

To learn more about hagfish, visit
www.bearportpublishing.com/Slime-inators

About the Author

Ellen Lawrence lives in the United Kingdom. Her favorite books to write are those about nature and animals. In fact, the first book Ellen bought for herself when she was six years old was the story of a gorilla named Patty Cake that was born in New York's Central Park Zoo.

Answer for Page 17

Hagfish are one of the ocean's recyclers. They eat the dead bodies of other animals, which helps to clean up the seabed.